Noble Dreams & Simple Pleasures

AMERICAN MASTERWORKS FROM MINNESOTA COLLECTIONS

By Sue Canterbury

MINNEAPOLIS INSTITUTE OF ARTS

Alexis Jean Fournier, 1865–1948, *In Daubigny's Country: Chaponval, France*, 1912, oil on canvas, MPB Collection

Acknowledgments

SHORTLY AFTER I ARRIVED IN MINNEAPOLIS in 1998, the seeds of what would become "Noble Dreams & Simple Pleasures" began to take root in my imagination. In my role as a curator, I had the good fortune to visit several Minnesota collectors of American art whose collections demonstrated a great deal of taste and discernment. As I learned of additional collectors, three things became apparent: no local exhibition celebrating the range of American art before modernism had ever occurred; the caliber of those works promised the makings of a visually rich exhibition; and the cumulative depth of the collections could effectively convey the story of American art before modernism.

I little anticipated the enthusiasm with which the lenders to this exhibition would furlough the "jewels" of their collections in a most generous effort to make this the best show possible. I was afraid I had asked one owner for too many works, but she rushed to assuage my worries. "Oh no," she assured me, "it's like having the children in the school play!" Clearly, for her and her fellow contributors, it is the art that they celebrate. And through their generosity they have allowed us to join in the fun. "Noble Dreams & Simple Pleasures" is an ideal opportunity for us all—the museum and community—to acknowledge what these collectors have accomplished through their love of art and their passion for the chase.

Many individuals have played key roles in making possible this presentation of "Noble Dreams & Simple Pleasures." The exhibition concept could not have been realized without the early endorsement of the MIA's former director and president, William M. Griswold, and the continuing support of the MIA's current director and president, Kaywin Feldman. For ensuring that the resources of the institution were marshaled behind this exhibition and catalogue, my thanks go to Matthew Welch and Laura DeBiaso. My colleagues in the Department of Paintings and Modern Sculpture (Patrick Noon, Erika Holmquist-Wall, Jane Satkowski, and Nicole Wankel) gave vital support, both moral and tangible, towards the success of this project. I am particularly grateful to Brian Kraft, Ken Krenz, Jennifer Starbright, and Lisa Ranallo in the Registration Department, who expended a great deal of time and thought in orchestrating the complex logistics associated with the transport of objects and scheduling of photography. My thanks also goes to Kurt Nordwall who, in support of the photography project, tirelessly unframed and reframed all the objects pictured within this book. That photography, and the quality thereof, is owed entirely to the expertise of Charles Walbridge, who captured the images with such precision, and Heidi Quicksilver, who fine-tuned their final digital presentation for purposes of public relations, marketing, and posting on the Web. My research for this project was given unstinting support from the MIA librarians, Janice Lurie and Jessica McIntyre.

Many individuals deserve a great deal of thanks for their contributions to the creation and presentation of the public face of "Noble Dreams & Simple Pleasures." On the most physical level, my sincere thanks go to Roxanne Ballard, for planning, in the most effective manner, the Target Gallery installation, and to the works-of-art crew for perfectly executing her plans. For her leadership as assistant director of institutional outreach, my thanks go to Leann Standish. In Design and Editorial, kudos go to Gayle Jorgens, for her direction in keeping us all on schedule; Jill Blumer, for her sensitive and brilliant design concepts for the catalogue and all public relations and marketing materials; Kristine Thayer, Elizabeth Mullen, and Diane Richard, for lending their time and expertise at various points along the way; and Jodie Ahern, who worked to sharpen and clarify my essays contained within this small tome. For their enthusiastic efforts in shining a light on our project to the press, sincere thanks go to Anne-Marie Wagener and Tammy Pleshek of Press and Public Relations. I am also grateful to Kristin Prestegaard and Ginnie O'Neill in Marketing and Communications for all they have done to ensure a sustained public profile during the run of the exhibition. Also key in maintaining that profile on the MIA Web site are James Ockuly, Michael Dust, Jennifer Jurgens, and Patrick Edwards of Interactive Media. Finally, for what promises to be memorable programming around the exhibition, I am indebted to Susan Jacobsen, Luke Erickson, and Julia Modest of Public Programs.

Outside of the museum, several individuals enthusiastically offered contacts that ultimately had an impact on the checklist for the exhibition. Key among those who opened doors to collectors unknown to me are Wes and Leon Kramer of Kramer Galleries, and Robert Quast. Similar suggestions were also forthcoming from some of the collectors themselves. Their advice has played a significant role in ensuring the remarkable breadth and depth of this exhibition. My sincere appreciation also goes to Jenny Sponberg and Taylor Acosta, of Curtis Galleries, for their generous assistance with the logistics of several loans.

"Noble Dreams & Simple Pleasures: American Masterworks from Minnesota Collections" is also indebted to the Minnesota State Arts Board for its generous grant, made possible through an appropriation by the Minnesota State Legislature and a grant from the National Endowment for the Arts. Such a gift is a tangible confirmation of their belief in the merits of the exhibition. Of course, this grant would not have been possible without the compelling grant application that was shaped and shepherded to completion by the MIA's grants specialist, Elisabeth Brandt. Sincere thanks also go to Larry and Barbara Braman Bentson for their generous support of this project. And last, but certainly not least, are our thanks for the liberal gift of funds from the MIA's Paintings Curatorial Council, which made publication of this catalogue a viable possibility.

Ultimately, neither this catalogue, nor the related exhibition would be possible without each of the thirty-one lenders whose names appear in the exhibition checklist at the end of this book. Their enthusiasm and overwhelming support for this project has been a study of generosity itself, even though that level of commitment dictates that their walls will remain bare for the duration of the exhibition. To each, I offer my utmost, heartfelt thanks for all they have contributed—tangible and intangible—during the course of this project. This exhibition belongs to them, each and every one.

—Sue Canterbury
Associate Curator of Paintings and Modern Sculpture
Minneapolis Institute of Arts

Herbjørn Gausta, 1854–1924, *Moonlit Scene* (detail), c. 1908, oil on canvas, private collection

Contents

Winslow Homer, 1836–1910, *Summer Night—Dancing by Moonlight*, 1890, oil on canvas, anonymous lender

Minnesota Collectors

IF JAMES J. HILL OR T. B. WALKER, the great art-collecting Minnesotans of the late nineteenth and early twentieth centuries, could cross the chasm of time to view the state of art collecting in Minnesota in the twenty-first century, they would be reassured. They would also be surprised to see how a pursuit that was mostly limited to the scions of family and industry in their era has been taken up by a passionate group of individuals spread over a wide range of occupations and socio economic levels. If Hill or Walker might not recognize or approve of some of the artistic styles that emerged during the years since their passing, they would, in the case of the present exhibition (which roughly covers American art before the advent of modernism),[1] find much that was familiar to them—even down to specific objects that were already in some Minnesota collections during their lifetimes.

Even though Hill focused his collecting activities primarily on French Barbizon paintings, he did acquire a few American works along the way.[2] Walker, on the other hand, cast a wide net and amassed Chinese jades (many now in the collection of the Minneapolis Institute of Arts), and European old-master paintings (those with religious subject matter now belong to the Hennepin Avenue Methodist Church). Moreover, Walker's remarkable selection of nineteenth-century American masterworks by artists such as Rembrandt Peale, Thomas Cole, Frederic Church, George Inness, and Thomas Moran[3] would have acquainted him with many of the artists featured in "Noble Dreams & Simple Pleasures."

Hill and Walker would also find much in common with the community spirit that has brought together works from the private collections of thirty-one Minnesotans. Both men realized what they had assembled held great value not just for themselves, but also for the greater community in which they lived. Consequently, each endeavored to make his collection accessible for the education and edification of his fellow citizens.[4] Each man's home was equipped with salon-style galleries that were comparable to those in any museum of the era. In contrast, the lenders to this exhibition live with their art on a more intimate scale, incorporating it into the very fabric of their daily lives, in every area of their homes. It is through bringing together the best from each of these homes that we are allowed to glimpse the fruits of each collector's labors, and experience the powerful visual sum of all their parts—collectively presented under ideal conditions and within their art historical context.

Many of the collectors represented in "Noble Dreams & Simple Pleasures" have found an aspect of American art that forms the whole, or at least the core, of their collections (e.g., Folk Art, Hudson River School, American Impressionism, or Minnesota Painters). Regardless of whether a collection focus is narrow or broad, certain factors determine the acquisition of a new work. Most obviously, an object must possess an overarching aesthetic combination (i.e., color, composition, paint application, and condition). Beyond this, a visceral response or gut reaction can be the ultimate, decisive factor. Other collectors can be more pragmatic or cerebral in their approach. Some may want their collections to reflect the depth of an artistic movement or school. Such a collector may possess works by artists A, B, D, and E, but won't rest until he or she acquires the right works by artists C and F. Additionally, some collectors are fascinated by all stages of a particular artist's career, and collect his or her works in depth, rather than limiting their purchases to a phase of work the market declares as being most desirable.

How would modern-day Minnesota collectors define themselves? First, many would be reluctant to define themselves as collectors. The very word "collector" carries a weight engendered by a burden of assumptions, not the least of which is that a collector must be rich, educated, and in possession of rarified knowledge about the artists, their schools, and the context surrounding their artistic production. In fact, nothing could be further from the truth.

It is the art objects themselves—the paintings, the sculptures, the drawings—that drive the collector's agenda. It is passion for these works of art that leads many of these individuals down a path some liken to an addiction (pleasant, but certainly habit-forming). Once they possess the prize, it is the object itself that compels these collectors to find out more about it, the artist, and the circumstances of its creation. Many repetitions later, they have amassed what someone else calls a "collection." It has simply crept up on them, unawares, while they were immersed in the love of the chase.

It is not unusual to find art collectors who have become experts in their areas of interest and who know their subject better than many curators (present author included). The desire for knowledge about their specific holdings launches many into research, leading quite a few into another limitless collecting area—the personal library. Similarly, collectors may invest much time and travel in visits to historical societies to scour documents for tidbits of information, or to make pilgrimages to an artist's home or favorite haunts. Some even visit the actual sites depicted in their paintings. It is all part of the process in which each collector can engage to the extent he or she chooses.

In talking with any collector, it becomes patently clear that a collection is never static. It is constantly growing and evolving. While some collections might be based on a core of inherited objects, the current generation has built upon it or broadened its boundaries. Those who began their collections decades ago—perhaps inadvertently—have noticed their tastes and interests shifting with experience, and consequently, their eye for quality growing sharper. This maturity has led some to change focus (leaving behind European art for American), or to "trade up" in quality for more important works by artists already in their collections. Thus, their early acquisitions often re-enter the market, to be adopted by other, future collectors. Collecting art, like tending a loved garden, requires constant refinement, turning the act of collecting into an art form in its own right.

Just as a collector is committed to the chase, he or she is committed to each object and its welfare. Accordingly, being a collector requires stewardship to assure that a work receives restorative measures when needed and that it is presented in his or her home in a manner that ensures its safety and physical stability (i.e., regulating exposures to light, heat, and humidity). Also key to many collectors is the role of the perfect frame. Thus, while collectors are proprietary about their collections, they all fully realize that they are just one link in a chain of many custodians who have passed these works on through time to the next generation of caretakers. In this sense, each collector is "owned" by the works they have so closely guarded and shepherded through time.

Finally, all of the collectors represented in "Noble Dreams & Simple Pleasures" hold in common two traits that have compelled them to participate in such a generous manner: a passion to share with others those objects that have so significantly enriched their lives and environments, and an overriding desire to share the richness and complexity of the American story conveyed through the most eloquent means possible. In effect, this visual feast is their gift to us.

Edward Kirkbride Thomas, 1817–1906, *View of Fort Snelling from Mendota*, 1851, oil on canvas, anonymous loan

Notes

1. The advent of modernism in America is generally linked to the staging of the "Armory Show" in New York in 1913. For most Americans, and many American artists, the Armory Show was the formal introduction of European modernism (i.e., Fauvism, French Cubism, Expressionism, etc.) in the United States.

2. As Hill's commitment to Barbizon painting deepened, he resold or exchanged his earliest acquisitions in an effort to refine his collection. The American works he acquired in 1883 and before were given to family and friends, as well as to local institutions such as the Minneapolis Public Library and the Minnesota Historical Society. See Sheila ffolliott, "James J. Hill as Art Collector: A Documentary View," in *Homecoming: The Art Collection of James J. Hill.* Saint Paul: Minnesota Historical Society Press (1991), p. 26.

3. These works were part of a group of fifteen 19th-century American paintings that were sold by the Walker Art Center at Sotheby's New York, May 24, 1989, to establish a purchase fund for contemporary art in the name of the donor (T. B. Walker Foundation).

4. Accessibility differed, though, between the two collections. From the opening of Walker's first one-room gallery in 1879 (the first public gallery in the Northwest), access was free to all. See Philip Larson, "Thomas Barlow Walker: From Private Collection to Public Art Center," in *Hennepin County History*, vol. 30, no. 4, spring 1971, p. 6. Hill was not as egalitarian. See Thomas O'Sullivan, "Showcase and Stronghold: The Art Gallery of the James J. Hill House," in *Homecoming*, pp. 56–57, who notes that "cards of admission" provided a space for noting the person who had introduced the visitor. One might extrapolate from this that the demographics of the visitors were thereby kept to the upper ranks of society.

Folk Art

FOR OVER A HALF-CENTURY (roughly 1760 to 1840), creative activity by untrained artists/artisans flourished in the United States. Their work enhanced the lives and captured the dreams of early Americans with a directness and simplicity that charms us today. While academically trained artists dominated artistic production in the major coastal cities such a Philadelphia and Boston, self-taught itinerant painters served the rising class of landowners, small businesspeople, and merchants who settled and prospered in the villages of rural America. Isolated by rugged terrain, these small communities sprang up along pre-existing Native American trails and waterways; the villages were accessible to only the most determined travelers. Arduous transport in cramped coaches over rutted roads, nights spent in flea-infested inns, and bad food were some of the hurdles itinerant peddlers and painters endured in their endeavors to locate and serve the rural consumers of their day.[1]

While folk painters could provide their clients with the occasional decorative still life, marine, or landscape painting, portraiture was the bread and butter of their existence. A new class of merchants and professionals was eager to affirm its status within the community. Some of these people found that simple, direct portraits most effectively broadcast their successes. While Calvinist principles eschewed luxury in any form, church ideology made exceptions for portraiture because these pictures honored the family. Displays of luxury items within a portrait also received a pardon from doctrine, because these material rewards were signifiers of one's piety—in that such things went to those who were in a "state of grace" with their creator.[2]

Graphic simplicity and standard poses and costumes were shortcuts that enabled the folk artist to maximize his/her modest fee with a minimal investment of time.[3] The accompanying props—dresses, cashmere shawls, and jewels for the ladies; ships and telescopes for former sea captains; Bibles for the village pastor; and expensive toys for the children—were elements of a succinct visual vocabulary employed to convey the sitter's status or profession. Even producing an accurate likeness took a back seat to emphasizing one's status for posterity, as in the case of Fitz-Green Halleck, who instructed his portraitist, Thomas Hicks:

I want you to paint me so that I shall look like a gentleman. Never mind the likeness. In fifty years nobody will be able to tell whether the portrait is a likeness or not; but I want to be handed down to posterity as a gentleman.[4]

The arrival of new technologies made such attitudes a thing of the past. Improved roads, new railways, and the availability of print media (i.e., magazines and journals) connected previously isolated communities to the larger world and to contemporary tastes and fashions. This heightened awareness transformed the expectations of the client and, in turn, demanded more sophisticated skills from the itinerant painter. Moreover, the introduction of photography, especially the daguerreotype, in the 1840s signaled the end to this early, golden era of folk art.

Notes

1. Harlan Lane, *A Deaf Artist in Early America: The Worlds of John Brewster, Jr.* Boston: Beacon Press (2004), pp. 22–23.

2. Lane, p. 24.

3. Realistic representations were time intensive and some artists, such as Matthew Prior, employed a sliding fee scale linked to the degree of finish desired. His fees ranged from $2 to $25. See Colleen Cowles Heslip, "Between the Rivers: The Rise and Fall of the Artisan Painter," in *Between the Rivers: Itinerant Painters from the Connecticut to the Hudson.* Ex. cat., Williamstown: Sterling and Francine Clark Art Institute, April 7 through July 22, 1990, p. 27, n. 19.

4. Heslip, p. 23.

Susan Catherine Moore Waters, 1823–1900, *Boy with Knife,* c. 1840–45, oil on canvas, collection of Stewart Stender and Deborah Davenport

William James Hubard, 1807–62, *Adam and Eve before the Fall,* c. 1840, oil on canvas, private collection

Joshua Johnson, 1765–1830, *Portrait of Richard John Cock,* c. 1815, oil on canvas, collection of Samuel D. and Patricia N. McCullough

Susanna Paine, 1792–1862, *Rhode Island Woman in White,* 1824,
pastel and applied gold foil on paper, collection of Stewart Stender
and Deborah Davenport

Thomas Chambers, 1808–69, *The Shipwreck,* 1850, oil on canvas, private collection

Capt. S. Eastman U.S. Army Delt.

Early Minnesota

THE WESTWARD EXPANSION of the United States during the first half of the nineteenth century generated explosive growth in the Minnesota Territories. Once the preserve of French voyageurs and fur traders who had forged collaborative working relationships with the native population, the region and its seemingly limitless natural resources (i.e., fertile prairies and virgin timberland) beckoned new waves of settlers seeking a new life and economic opportunity. The Mississippi was both barrier and doorstep, and Fort Snelling, established at the confluence of the Mississippi and Minnesota (then called St. Peters) rivers, was a government foothold in the vast expanse that stretched north and west.

A need for geographic and topographic information, together with an overarching curiosity about the region and its inhabitants, propelled a succession of adventurous draftsmen and artists eager to be the region's first visual interpreters. Key among the landscape painters were J. F. Kensett, Alfred Thompson Bricher, Albert Bierstadt, Ferdinand Reichardt, and Robert S. Duncanson. Earlier painters documented the native peoples and customs, most notably George Catlin, Charles Bodmer, Seth Eastman, John Mix Stanley, Edward Thomas, and Frank B. Mayer. Traditional native life was already under siege from government incursion into Indian affairs and lands. It was only a matter of time—a very short time—until life as the native people knew it would be irretrievably lost.

Indeed, Minnesota at mid-century was a place caught up in rapid transition on several levels, particularly sociological and economic. Clearly, the commercial harvesting of lumber was the chief catalyst to such accelerated change. The forests east of the Mississippi had gradually been harvested and tapped out. Minnesota offered new stands of virgin forest and a waterway—the Mississippi—that made lumber's conveyance to mill and market economically efficient.[1] Inevitably, the service industries that grew up to support logging transformed the unspoiled settings adjacent to the river. For instance, settlement on the west bank of St. Anthony Falls went from one house in 1850 to a whole town (Minneapolis) by 1859, and sawmills, foundries, shingle machines, and lath factories operated at full tilt.[2] Such rapid changes fascinated artists, photographers, and the public alike in the second half of the century, as evidence of a march toward progress through the civilization of untamed land and the harnessing of nature's seemingly limitless power.

The images left behind by all the artists who sought to document Minnesota offer us all a virtual window to the past through which it is possible to glimpse the foreshadowing of our present, unmediated by the alterations of time, commerce, and changing tastes of the intervening years.

Notes

1. Michael Conforti, "Introduction: Art and Life on the Upper Mississippi 1890–1915," in *Minnesota 1900: Art and Life on the Upper Mississippi 1890–1915.* Ex. cat., Minneapolis Institute of Arts. Newark: University of Delaware Press (199__), p. 13.

2. Janet L. Whitmore, "A Panorama of Unequaled Yet Ever-Varying Beauty," in *Currents of Change: Art and Life along the Mississippi River 1850–1861.* Ex. cat., Minneapolis Institute of Arts (2004), p. 25. The lone house belonged to Helen and John Stevens.

Seth Eastman, 1808–75, *Laughing Waters, Three Miles Below the Falls of St. Anthony*, n.d., watercolor, from the Seth Eastman Collection, sponsored by Nivin S. MacMillan

Seth Eastman, 1808–75, *The Falls of St. Anthony*, 1848, oil on canvas, anonymous lender

James Desvarreaux-Larpenteur, 1847–1937, *The Gibbs Homestead*, c. 1880, oil on canvas, private collection

Grafton Tyler Brown, 1841–1918, *Mississippi at Winona*, c. 1894, oil on canvas, collection of Daniel Shogren and Susan Meyer

Barton Stone Hays, 1826–1914, *First Mills on the Mississippi and Spirit Island, c. 1857*, c. 1880s, oil on canvas, anonymous lender

A National Art: Landscape, Still Life, and Genre

WHILE THE EIGHTEENTH CENTURY WITNESSED an America with one foot in European culture, the nineteenth brought about a period of self-discovery and coming of age for the young nation. Cultural optimism and the expectation of greatness predominated the imagery of the age. Sumptuous still lifes with allusions to abundance, and anecdotal genre scenes celebrating the simple joys and values of the common folk were the idealized visual documents of democratic America. But in considering the century's artistic output, it is the enduring landscape tradition that clarifies the close link between love of land and the formation of the American identity.

America's vast expanse of available land was a beacon of adventure and opportunity to all who were willing to brave the dangers of the wilderness and shoulder the hard work required to settle it. The nation's natural wonders seemed uniquely American in scope and visual splendor. Europe had its castles and cathedrals from bygone centuries, but America embodied the future—full of limitless natural resources and picturesque wonders, such as Niagara Falls, the Rocky Mountains, Yosemite Valley, the mighty Mississippi River, and the Grand Canyon. The Hudson River School painters gave visual expression to the nationalistic belief in America's "manifest destiny," which professed that any country so abundantly blessed was divinely ordained for greatness.

Roughly spanning the years from 1820 to 1870, the Hudson River School dominated artistic production in the United States. Although considered the first truly American school of art, its stylistic roots were connected to European aesthetic theories of the romantic sublime and the picturesque landscape. In essence, these concepts held that the landscape's purpose was to convey nature's immensity, power, and drama, thereby registering overwhelming awe or fear in the beholder. The enormity of the American landscape was well suited to such concepts. To depict them, artists used dynamic compositional formulas, detailed realism, high contrasts of light and dark, and bravura manipulation of atmospheric light effects.

During the half-century in which the school held sway, the highly idealized landscape came to share the stage with more naturalistic representations, wherein the subject matter (nature) was allowed to speak for itself. Central to any portrayal, however, was the group's dedication to direct observation. Accordingly, each went in search of his or her visual quarry— camping and hiking in the Adirondacks, the Catskills, and the White Mountains of New Hampshire, and eventually exploring the Mississippi and beyond. Their goal was to capture the expanding nation's scenery in sketches to be worked up in larger, fully finished canvases back at their studios.

It was during the third quarter of the century that several artists' depictions of the nation's lakes, rivers, and coastal waters rose to a lyrical and spiritual crescendo that, unlike the romantic sublime prized earlier in the century, elicited a more contemplative response. Through a deft manipulation of paint, artists portrayed water, reflections, and atmospheric light to stunning effect in what has come to be called Luminism. The combination of sharply delineated forms, imperceptible brushstrokes, and carefully edited compositional components, when cast in a luminous, veiled light, became a hymn to visual perfection through which the viewer transcended earthbound materiality and concerns.[1]

The carnage of the Civil War acted like blight on the American soul, and the disillusionment that followed squelched the optimism and the patriotic fervor of the preceding years. The art of that era was deemed naïve and its artists, consequently, fell out of favor. It was only with the passage of time and

Robert Scott Duncanson, 1821–72, *Still Life with Fruit and Nuts*, 1848, oil on canvas, private collection

generations that the importance of the these artists and their work was resurrected from obscurity and re-evaluated in terms of its technical mastery and as the expression of an era so imbued with the American dream.

Notes

1. Transcendentalist belief in the existence of a universal soul shared by humans, nature, and God (as promulgated by Ralph Waldo Emerson), influenced some of these artists. This theory reached back to the 18th-century Calvinist theologian, Jonathan Edwards, who saw the universal soul as a fusion of beauty, truth, and virtue through a "divine and supernatural light." See Douglas J. Elwood, *The Philosophical Theology of Jonathan Edwards*. New York: Columbia University Press (1960), vii.

Alvan Fisher, 1792–1863, *Approaching Storm, White Mountains*, c. 1820s, oil on canvas, anonymous lender

Asher Brown Durand, 1796–1886, *Genesee Valley, New York State*, c. 1850, oil on canvas, anonymous lender

George Inness, 1825–94, *Landscape with Sheep*, 1858, oil on canvas, private collection

George Loring Brown, 1814–89, *The Crown of New England*, 1863, oil on canvas, collection of Alfred and Ingrid Lenz Harrison

William Stanley Haseltine, 1835–1900, *Off Newport Island*, 1863, oil on canvas, Burrichter-Kierlin Collection at the Minnesota Marine Art Museum, Winona, Minnesota

Eastman Johnson, 1824–1906, *Sugaring Off*, 1863, oil on canvas, private collection

William Trost Richards, 1833–1905, *Nantucket Bluffs*, 1866, oil on canvas, collection of Douglas and Mary Olson

Severin Roesen, 1815–72, *Fruit Still Life*, c. 1860s, oil on canvas, collection of Douglas and Mary Olson

Joseph Rusling Meeker, 1827–89, *Bayou*, n.d.,
oil on canvas, private collection

Jervis McEntee, 1828–91, *Lake Placid—Adirondac*,
1868, oil on canvas, private collection

Alfred Thompson Bricher, 1837–1908, *Mississippi River (Dubuque, Iowa)*, 1870, oil on canvas, Burrichter-Kierlin Collection at the Minnesota Marine Art Museum, Winona, Minnesota

George Inness, 1825–94, *View near Rome*, 1871, oil on canvas, collection of John and Elizabeth Driscoll

Worthington Whittredge, 1820–1910, *The Club House Sitting Room at Balsam Lake, Catskills, New York*, 1886, oil on canvas, collection of Eleanor and Fred Winston

The Transatlantics: Cosmopolitanism, Expatriates, and American Impressionism

FROM AMERICA'S EARLIEST DAYS, its art and politics were related symbiotically, wherein the one was expressed through the other. The mandate to the American artist was that his or her work should have a distinctively American character. The idealized landscape—even though indebted to European models—had been hailed at first as the fulfillment of such a mandate. But in the nineteenth century, the development of art schools, competitions, and salons in America was in its infancy. Aware of this, those artists able to do so sought training abroad in an effort to improve their technical skills and to study past masterpieces and contemporary trends. This trickle of transatlantic traffic would turn into a flood in the wake of the 1867 Universal Exposition in Paris. The negative criticism rained down upon works of the American school—which were almost entirely idealized landscapes—would force the nation to step back and reassess the state of the arts in the United States.

During the majority of the nineteenth century, the academies of Rome, Düsseldorf, and Munich had been the primary destinations for American artists seeking formal training. In the wake of the American Civil War, Paris had emerged as the new capital of the art world, where a budding artist could choose among myriad teachers and trends.[1] An artist with a classicist bent could train under Jean-Léon Gérôme. Thomas Couture, the master of realism, could mentor another. Many Americans who were denied entry to the official school—École des Beaux Arts—could find a welcome at the Académie Julian. Also available was the study of the nude—mastery of which was essential for advancement under the French system. And advance they must if these American artists were to achieve their ultimate goal of gaining admittance to the yearly Salon. If American artists made it there, they were reasonably assured of making it anywhere.

Alongside this incoming and outgoing tide of American artists to Paris in the last quarter of the century were the expatriate American artists who had achieved acclaim within their own artistic specialties. Each was celebrated for his or her success, and was, consequently, highly influential on compatriot artists back home. Mary Cassatt of Philadelphia had put down roots in Paris and actively exhibited with the French Impressionists at the Salon des Indépendants. She was also an active promoter of Impressionist art to American collectors. New England-born James Abbott McNeill Whistler was active on both sides of the English Channel, and the acquisition of his work by the French government was viewed as a victory for American art in general.

In contrast to these native-born Americans was John Singer Sargent, born in Europe to expatriate Americans. He first visited his parents' country in 1876, when he was twenty years of age, to claim his American citizenship. Regardless, Sargent's critical successes at the Paris Salons and commercial success as a portraitist were viewed as proof of America's advancing status in the arts.

European art colonies, such as those at Pont-Aven and Barbizon (near the Forest of Fontainebleau), offered Americans additional opportunities to experiment with stylistic trends and subject matter not favored by the academic masters. Beginning in the 1880s, another art colony, Giverny, began to grow in popularity, in part because it offered new scenery, but more so because of its famous resident, Claude Monet. While the French master never acted as a teacher to any of the new arrivals, his presence and artistic practice (i.e., *plein air* painting

Robert Lewis Reid, 1862–1929, *Girl at Window*, 1885, oil on canvas, collection of Siri and Bob Marshall

James Abbott McNeill Whistler, 1834–1903, *The Seashore*, 1883–85, oil on panel, anonymous lender

and the Impressionist color palette) certainly influenced the overall artistic spirit of the village. The first wave of Americans who arrived in 1886 and 1887 included Theodore Robinson, Willard Metcalf, John Leslie Breck, Dawson Dawson-Watson, Theodore Wendel, and Theodore Butler (who married Monet's daughter, Suzanne).[2] Among the last to decamp with the advent of World War I were Richard Miller and Frederick Frieseke.

In spite of all the newly acquired credentials from study in European academies and art colonies, and the validation of exhibiting at the Salons, American artists returning from "bohemia" to the United States found new challenges to overcome. On one hand, the new aristocracy of wealth in the United States passed over European-trained American artists for their French contemporaries. On the other hand, many conservative Americans—the public and critics alike—

clamored for art that was undeniably American in its subject matter and its manner of execution, considering the returning American artists as being "too French" in their views and training. Many artists had to learn to negotiate these shoals of public taste and prejudice; some were more successful than others.

Notes

1. The number of American artists matriculating in French academies accelerated after 1870 (the close of the Franco-Prussian War). In 1888, one thousand Americans were registered as art students in Paris. See Kathleen Adler, "We'll Always Have Paris: Paris as Training Ground and Proving Ground," in *Americans in Paris: 1860–1900*. Ex. cat., London: National Gallery Company Limited (2006), p. 11.

2. Monet moved to Giverny in 1883. See Katherine M. Bourguignon, "Giverny: A Village for Artists," in *Impressionist Giverny: A Colony of Artists, 1885–1915*. Ex. cat., Giverny: Terra Foundation for American Art (2007), pp. 17–19, n. 4. While Sargent never aligned himself officially with the Impressionists, he and Claude Monet were friends from the 1880s onward. The American spent several successive summers at Giverny.

Walter Launt Palmer, 1854–1932, *Blue-Barred Snow*, 1888, oil on canvas, collection of Alfred and Ingrid Lenz Harrison

Theodore Robinson, 1852–96, *Normandy Farm*, c. 1891, oil on canvas, collection of Michael and Jean Antonello

Walter Launt Palmer, 1854–1932, *Lagoon of Venice*, 1895, oil on canvas, private collection

George Hitchcock, 1850–1913, *Swans by a Bridge, Holland*, 1898, oil on canvas, collection of Siri and Bob Marshall

Theodore Earl Butler, 1861–1936, *On the Seine*, 1902, oil on canvas, private collection

John Singer Sargent, 1856–1925, *Val d'Aosta: Stepping Stones*, c. 1907, oil on canvas, collection of Michael and Jean Antonello

John Singer Sargent, 1856–1925, *The Moraine*, 1908, oil on canvas, private collection

Edmund Charles Tarbell, 1862–1938, *Portrait of Mercie Tarbell*, c. 1919,
oil on canvas, private collection

Tonalism

BECAUSE AMERICAN IMPRESSIONISM is so widely admired today, it is difficult to fathom that its acceptance in the United States was not immediate, and its future success not a foregone conclusion.[1] Its tenuous beginnings were due, in great part, to another stylistic movement—today known as Tonalism—that had already established a foothold in American critical circles by the time repatriated American artists introduced their domesticated version of Impressionism. A continuous insistence that U.S. art should be unmistakably American in subject and spirit caused American Impressionism to be judged a fleeting fad and the spawn of dubious French upstarts. Ironically, Tonalism was touted as a uniquely American invention, even though its ancestral roots also extended to French soil—albeit further back to the Barbizon School. This relationship to a familiar and accepted tradition that had already been "Americanized" by a previous generation helped predispose American audiences to the tonalist artists and their work.[2]

A key force in forming and codifying the tenets of Tonalism was the artist George Inness. While associated with the Hudson River School, Inness had encountered the Barbizon aesthetic in France in the 1850s, and signs of the cultivated landscape (an integral aspect of that French movement) began to appear in his work shortly thereafter. It wasn't until the mid-1870s, however, that Inness sowed the first seeds of Tonalism. His new experiments on the Barbizon model suppressed detail and evoked mood and nostalgia, developing into what was critically termed the "suggestive landscape." By the late 1880s, this expressive stylistic approach became the virtual definition of a movement and Inness, its creator, the magnet to a coterie of followers.[3]

American acceptance of Tonalism was advanced by an awareness of the lyrical works of the infamous American expatriate, James Abbott McNeill Whistler. While Whistler never aligned himself with the group, his elegantly ambiguous compositions of color "nocturnes" and his "arrangements" in narrow ranges of tones served as inspirations. The aesthetic purposes of Whistler and the Tonalists, however, were distinctly different. Whistler was chiefly concerned with achieving pictorial perfection—art for art's sake. The tonalist objective rested in evoking a personal response to nature—something Whistler would have rejected outright as "pure claptrap."[4]

In formal terms, Tonalism was a rejection of the grandiose God's-eye-view wilderness landscapes of the Hudson River School that had preceded it. Yet it was a continuation of America's love affair with the land. While indebted to the Barbizon aesthetic of the cultivated pastoral landscape, the tonalist artists relied on abstraction through concentration on fragments of landscape that, while familiar, were never specifically identifiable.[5] These anonymous landscapes, with nebulous titles linked to times of day or season, were meant to trigger the imagination of the viewer. As such, many works were based on the slightest of on-site sketches, or were completely reliant on an artist's recollections. Therefore, the finished canvases generally were pure studio productions with an emphasis on craftsmanship. The rich color, the narrow gradations of tone, the blurring of forms, and the complex and highly finished surfaces employed by these artists coalesced into canvases imbued with a meditative spirituality.[6]

The creation of such soulfulness was heavily indebted to the processes and techniques of the style. The smoky *sfumato* effects were achieved through a complicated layering of thin glazes built up in many stages. Glazes were composed of pigment mixed into a suspension of either oil or varnish, which allowed light to penetrate down to a color ground layer that, for many Tonalists, was the warm yellow of sunshine.[7] Using cool-toned glazes over a warm-toned ground layer was essential

Benjamin Foster, 1852–1926, *Connecticut Landscape*, n.d., oil on canvas, lent by Paul and Barbara Watkins

in achieving the luminous, atmospheric effects so characteristic of this school of painters.[8]

By the turn of the century, tonalist painters had become both critically and financially successful. Although the original members (Inness, Alexander Wyant, and Homer Dodge Martin) had passed on, a younger generation rose to carry the movement forward. Their exhibitions at the Lotos Club in New York City (which became the premier promotional venue of the school) were hailed for their unified, harmonious effects. And in an early example of "branding," the Tonalists officially organized and exhibited in 1899 as the "Society of American Landscape Painters." When several Tonalists were recognized and rewarded at the Universal Exposition of 1900 in Paris, they felt the movement was validated as a truly authentic, American style of landscape painting.[9]

In spite of its success, Tonalism's time in the spotlight was short. By 1905 it was being eclipsed by the American Impressionists as well as the gritty, urban aesthetic of the young painters of the Ashcan School. The number of core exhibitors gradually thinned and by 1920 the movement had fully passed into its twilight. Ironically, the very aspects that had led to the success of the movement (i.e., nostalgic images looking back as if to some lost age) led to its demise. In spite of its visual poetry, Tonalism's countless repetitions of variations on the same theme were not ultimately sustainable.

Notes

1. Key American collectors resisted Impressionism during the 1890s and early 20th century, preferring the muted landscapes of the Tonalist painters. See Jack Becker, "Lotos Club," in *The Poetic Vision: American Tonalism*. New York: Spanierman Gallery (2005), p. 32.

2. By the 1880s, exhibitions of works by the French Barbizon masters and their American acolytes were quite common in major American cities. See William H. Gerdts, "American Tonalism: An Artistic Overview," in *The Poetic Vision: American Tonalism*, p. 22.

3. Nicolai Cikovsky, Jr., "George Inness and Tonalist Uncertainty," in *The Poetic Vision: American Tonalism*, p. 52.

4. Linda Merrill, "The Soul of Refinement: Whistler and American Tonalism," in *The Poetic Vision: American Tonalism,* pp. 68–69.

5. See Gerdts, p. 15.

6. Many critics viewed Impressionism's emphasis on materiality (i.e., its unfinished sketchiness, garish color, and impastoed surfaces) as an absence of spiritual value. See Gerdts, p. 23.

7. See Lance Mayer and Gay Myers, "Understanding the Techniques of American Tonalist and Impressionist Painters," in *Journal of the American Institute for Conservation,* vol. 32, no. 2 (summer 1993), pp. 129–139.

8. The practice of using varnish as a suspension medium has also been the undoing of many a tonalist painting by restorers who, seeking to remove yellowed varnish, unwittingly removed the thin, delicate glazes essential to the ultimate effect of the image.

9. Medals went to Charles Warren Eaton, Ben Foster, Birge Harrison, and Albert Pinkham Ryder. One of the most recognized of the artists was Ralph Blakelock, whose only award in his lifetime was given him at Paris. See Diane P. Fischer, "Constructing the 'American School' of 1900," in *Paris 1900: The "American School" at the Universal Exposition.* Ex. cat., New Brunswick, N.J.: Rutgers University Press (1999), p. 81.

George Inness, 1825–94, *The Triumph at Calvary*, c. 1874, oil on canvas, collection of Andrew Fuller

John Francis Murphy, 1853–1921, *Afternoon Light*, 1887, oil on canvas, collection of John and Elizabeth Driscoll

Alexander Helwig Wyant, 1836–92, *Clouds and Sunshine*, n.d., oil on canvas, collection of John and Elizabeth Driscoll

George Inness, 1825–94, *Two Rainbows, Montclair*, 1892, oil on canvas, collection of Daniel T. and Helen E. Lindsay

William Crothers Fitler, 1857–1915, *Sunset Hour (New York Landscape)*, n.d., oil on canvas, collection of Billie Lawton

Dwight William Tryon, 1849–1925, *Early Moonrise—October*, 1913–14, oil on canvas, collection of Douglas and Mary Olson

Minnesota Painters

ART IN MINNESOTA DURING the second and third quarters of the nineteenth century concentrated mostly on factual documentation. Artists such as George Catlin, Seth Eastman, and Frank Mayer raced to create visual records of the region's unspoiled landscape and its native people before all was lost to the merciless march of time. By the 1870s, however, the burgeoning lumber and milling industries fueled a rise in affluence that sparked new hopes and visions for the region, emphasizing quality of life and cultural viability. A new quest for aesthetic beauty promoted the pursuit of art for the good of heart, mind, soul, and society.[1]

Before the turn of the century, Minnesota's art culture was centered in Minneapolis and was a very modest pursuit, initially championed by the ladies of local society. The city's first art exhibition, comprising works from Minnesota collections, opened in September 1878, and within four years, articles of incorporation were drafted for the Minneapolis Society of Fine Arts. Officially founded in January 1883, the society made clear from the outset an intention to advance the love of art through exhibitions and lectures. Most important, though, for the growth of an art culture, was the goal of establishing permanent facilities for the exhibition and study of art. The future role of art in Minneapolis was secured at the opening of the Minneapolis School of Art (today's Minneapolis College of Art and Design) in April 1886, under the direction of Stephen A. Douglas Volk.[2] However, it was Robert Koehler, the school's second director, arriving in 1893, who built a solid foundation in the city for both the practice and appreciation of fine art.[3]

Paralleling activities in Minneapolis were the efforts of various cities around the state, as they set up their own arts organizations. The St. Paul School of Fine Arts was established in 1894, evolving into the St. Paul Institute of Arts and Sciences after the turn of the century.[4] Although short-lived, New Ulm's art school opened in 1892. To the north, Duluth founded its own Art Institute in 1907.[5]

Integral to promoting artistic output in Minnesota were opportunities for exhibition—a means by which artists could gain exposure to the broader public while also gauging their progress among peers. Several artist organizations, such as the Minneapolis Art League (founded and led by Koehler), and the Chalk and Chisel Club (which later became the Arts & Crafts Society), provided exhibition opportunities. By the 1880s, some commercial venues also opened to area artists, including the Stevens and Robertson galleries in St. Paul and, in Minneapolis, the Beard Gallery and John S. Bradstreet's Crafthouse.[6] The Minnesota State Fair and, from 1886 through 1893, the Minneapolis Industrial Exposition served as large-scale exhibition platforms. The latter also exposed local artists and the public to works by a range of artists, from the old masters to contemporary Europeans and Americans. After the turn of the century, annual exhibitions by the Minneapolis Society of Fine Arts and the State Art Commission continued to serve the needs of the growing arts communities around the state.[7]

In spite of these local opportunities for education and exhibition, it was a professional rite of passage for Minnesota's aspiring artists (and their peers across America) to seek increased levels of training in other major cities. Some studied at the Art Institute of Chicago or the Pennsylvania Academy of Fine Arts in Philadelphia. However, the majority studied in New York at the Art Students League or the National Academy of Design. For those fortunate enough to have the means (or a sponsor), study in one of the academies of Europe was the ultimate goal. Although many of the artists returned to Minnesota to practice their profession, some failed to find necessary commercial support and departed to pursue professional fulfillment elsewhere.[8] It remained a sad truth

Robert Koehler, 1850–1917, *Stoney Point, Lake Ida* (Douglas County, Minnesota), c. 1900, oil on canvas, private collection

that Minnesota did not always render to its own artists the same respect and support they gave to artists situated on the East Coast or in Europe.[9] However, those artists who chose to establish themselves in Minnesota became the mentors who shaped the artists of a new generation and continued to build upon the legacy of their artistic forebears.

When viewed through the lens of state history, arts education, exhibitions, and commerce gained the support of a growing frontier community with extraordinary speed. Such an achievement was made possible only through the unflagging efforts of visionaries, and the support of citizens who saw the viability of their communities closely linked to the aesthetic enrichment of their environment. It is to these prescient individuals that the Minnesotans of today, who benefit from the art museums, art schools, commercial galleries, and an extensive artist community, owe a great debt of gratitude.

Notes

1. Michael Conforti, "Introduction: Art and Life on the Upper Mississippi 1890–1915," in *Minnesota 1900: Art and Life on the Upper Mississippi 1890–1915*. Newark: University of Delaware Press (1994), p. 16.

2. Roy A. Boe, *The Development of Art Consciousness in Minneapolis and the Problems of the Indigenous Artist.* Master thesis. University of Minnesota (1947), pp. 6–16. Unless noted otherwise, all information in this essay relies on Boe's scholarship.

3. Koehler was indefatigable in his support of the arts in Minneapolis. During his 24 years in the city, he served as director of the School of Art, founded and led the Art League, served as president of the Minnesota State Arts Commission (beginning in 1903), and edited the Bulletin for the Minneapolis Institute of Arts. The Society's annual exhibitions were also under his direction and he used that forum to expose the public and artists alike to the best of contemporary artistic practice.

4. Prior to establishment of St. Paul School of Art, Douglas Volk had been teaching art classes in the city, a practice he took over from Charles Noel Flagg (1848–1916), who returned to New York in 1887.

5. Thomas O'Sullivan, "Robert Koehler and Painting in Minnesota, 1890–1915," in Conforti, ed., *Art and Life on the Upper Mississippi: 1890–1915.* Ex. cat., pp. 93–121. In addition, the author notes the establishment of art interest groups that met on a regular basis in the cities of Faribault, Red Wing, Winona, and Moorhead.

6. O'Sullivan, p. 98.

7. O'Sullivan, p. 99. State law required the exhibitions of the State Art Commission/Society to be held in a different city every year in an effort to decentralize artistic opportunities.

8. See Rena Coen, *Minnesota Impressionists.* Afton, Minnesota: Afton Historical Society Press (c. 1996), who notes the departure of several artists for greener pastures. David Ericson of Duluth spent most of his career between Europe and Provincetown (pp. 38–40). Alexis Fournier relocated to East Aurora, New York, to teach and work with the Roycroft Community, later living in Brown County, Indiana. He maintained a home in Minneapolis for many years and continued to visit and exhibit here for most of his career (pp. 42–44). After returning to the state for a couple of years, Alexander Grinager relocated to the New York area in 1896, where he remained for the rest of his life (pp. 51–53). Even artists who had come from elsewhere to foster the arts in Minnesota suffered from lack of commercial support. See Boe (p. 17), who notes that Douglas Volk's departure was connected to the lack of local portrait commissions needed to supplement his salary as director of the school in Minneapolis. Returning to New York in 1893, he quickly secured both professional recognition and financial success. See O'Sullivan (p. 107), who writes that Robert Koehler, in the view of many, sacrificed his professional career by remaining in Minneapolis to do "missionary work for art."

9. O'Sullivan (p. 107) notes that Minnesota artists were not accorded the same respect given to their peers situated on the East Coast and in Europe. He cites in particular how East Coast artists were awarded the decorative commissions for the new State Capitol.

Alexis Jean Fournier, 1865–1948, *Old Mill Ruins at Pine Island, Minnesota*, c. 1885–86, oil on artist board, collection of Jeffrey C. Meehan

Alexis Jean Fournier, 1865–1948, *Old Row* (Fort Snelling) *from the Station, July 1888*, 1888, oil on canvas, anonymous lender

Nicholas Richard Brewer, 1857–1949, *At the Spring*, c. 1895, oil on canvas, promised gift of Rob P. Stock in memory of his parents, Philip E. and Mary C. (Mathewson) Stock

Herbjørn Gausta, 1854–1924, *Moonlit Scene*, c. 1908, oil on canvas, private collection

Nicholas Richard Brewer, 1857–1949, *The Shadow of the Grove*, 1910, oil on canvas, collection of Stephen J. Brewer

Alexander Grinager, 1865–1949, *The Fountain*, n.d., oil on canvas, collection of Sheila Morgan

Maurice Brazil Prendergast, 1858–1924, *Elegant Woman in Blue Dress*, c. 1893–94, watercolor and pencil on paper, Antonello Family Foundation

On the Cusp of Modernism

IN THE FIRST DECADE OF THE TWENTIETH century in America, many aesthetic styles uncomfortably co-existed as they struggled for critical and commercial success. Tonalism was slipping off its pedestal and slowly playing itself out. Conversely, American Impressionism was finding the public acceptance that had eluded the movement for so long. Its practitioners, at one time the avant-garde, had matured and were quickly becoming part of the mainstream establishment that had previously held them at bay. Into this mix of waxing and waning popularity stepped the young turks of a new generation determined to set itself apart from the dictates of tradition. This new vision would, over the course of a few years, break with the past and form a bridge to the future and modernism.[1] Nevertheless, during that first decade each aesthetic faction—traditional and progressive—struggled for the same narrow beam of spotlight.

Until the late nineteenth century, the annual exhibitions held in New York by the National Academy of Design ("NAD" or "Academy") and the Society of American Artists (a one-time renegade offshoot of the Academy) had provided the chief opportunities for artists to show their work. By the 1890s, however, the selection processes in both the NAD and the Society had become so conservative that innovative artists felt compelled to create their own associations and exhibition opportunities. The Tonalists began exhibiting together at the Lotus Club in 1895, and then formally gathered under the banner of "The Society of American Landscape Painters" in 1898. The American Impressionists similarly packaged themselves as "The Ten" in 1897 in an effort to secure independent exhibition venues. The struggle for exhibition space in New York was exacerbated in 1898 and '99 when the NAD sold and vacated its premises in anticipation of building a new facility. While annual exhibitions continued in temporary spaces, the destruction of

NAD's building by fire in 1905, along with the formal merger of the NAD and the Society in April 1906, tightly cinched the conduit of access through which emerging artists had to pass.[2]

Breaking the institutional conventions that predominated in New York required creative solutions from determined visionaries. Photographer Alfred Stieglitz sought to instigate change from outside the system as he championed photography as a fine art. He opened the Little Galleries of the Photo-Secession at 291 Fifth Avenue in 1902 in an act of rebellion that in one stroke put the public on notice that change was underway. It also distanced him and his pictorialist colleagues—Edward Steichen, Gertrude Käsebier, Clarence White, and others—from the more pedestrian mainstream fare of the New York Camera Club.[3] His gallery provided a venue in which effective presentation of the sympathetic works of the exhibitors underscored their status as fine art. Stieglitz's progressive agenda would soon expose New York and America to the leading edge of American avant-garde art by such painters as John Marin and Marsden Hartley.

Another vital faction in overturning the exhibition hegemony of the NAD was a coterie of artists who became known as "The Eight" (and later, the "Ashcan School"). They rejected the polished execution and genteel subject matter esteemed by the Academy. Instead, they dedicated themselves to capturing the gritty realities of daily life among the common classes, and their coarse subjects, decried by the critics, seemed materially matched to the raw manner of their execution. Their imagery emanated a sense of immediacy and vitality that grasped the viewer's attention, much in the manner of contemporary illustrations in the popular press. This similarity was no accident. Out of the eight artists who formed the Ashcan School, four—John Sloan, William Glackens, Everett Shinn, and George Luks—began their working careers in Philadelphia as newspaper artists before studying art with Robert Henri, who became the recognized leader of The Eight.[4] These artists set a new precedent for harnessing the power of the popular press to keep them before the public eye and to advocate for their work as true American art. The press sensationally branded them the new radicals and "men of rebellion."[5]

In contrast to the aesthetic homogeneity of the still-active American Impressionists and Tonalists, the exhibitions of The Eight appeared to be a gathering of strange bedfellows. Henri was well trained and his sophisticated technique stood in contrast to the gritty realism of Glackens, Luks, Shinn, and Sloan, as their work did against the dream-like classicism of Arthur B. Davies, the Impressionist landscapes of Ernest Lawson, and the French Nabis-inspired works of Maurice Prendergast.[6] While this unification of diverse styles was a realistic reflection of aesthetic variety of the period, for The Eight it was also an example of the democratic exhibition practices they had repeatedly urged the tradition-bound Academy to embrace. The NAD's intransigence, however, led the artists to explore increasingly creative options that ultimately revolutionized conceptions—for artists and the public alike—of what a progressive modern exhibition could be.[7] Consequently, it comes as no surprise that many of these artists were integral to the planning and staging of the ground-breaking Armory Show of 1913.

The ultimate irony of the Armory Show is that many of the artists—the American avant-garde of the first decade of the twentieth century—who helped to introduce European modernism to the American public, were eclipsed by the very exhibition they helped to mount. The realism of their work, in comparison to the abstractions of Cubism, and the exclamatory colors of Expressionism, seemed conservative by contrast. Regardless, it was their tireless work that shifted the very

foundations of a system previously unwilling to embrace the forces of change. We realize today that those pioneers forged a revolutionary path for art in the new American century.

Notes

1. The arrival of modernism in the United States is generally linked with the staging of the Armory Show in New York City in 1913 when the public and artists alike first experienced European modernism.

2. See Elizabeth Milroy, *Painters of a New Century: The Eight & American Art.* Ex. cat., Milwaukee Art Museum (1991), pp. 21–22.

3. Stieglitz's use of the term "secession" was clearly linked to contemporary aesthetic movements in Germany and Austria. In America, however, the word was freighted with negativity because of its association with the Civil War (Milroy, p. 44). Participating photographers were Edward Steichen, Gertrude Käsebier, Clarence White, and F. Holland Day, among others.

4. Edward Lucie-Smith, *American Realism.* London: Thames & Hudson Ltd. (1994), p. 71.

5. Milroy, pp. 27–28.

6. Milroy, p. 46.

7. In 1910, the group rented an empty house on West 35th Street in New York. Walt Kuhn, Guy Pène du Bois, Rockwell Kent, and Stuart Davis participated in planning and staging the exhibition. See Milroy, p. 88.

John Marin, 1870–1953, *Region Weehauken, New Jersey*, 1903–4, oil on canvas, collection of John and Elizabeth Driscoll

George Wesley Bellows, 1882–1925, *Upper Broadway*, 1907, oil on board, collection of Michael and Jean Antonello

Marsden Hartley, 1877–1943, *An Evening Mountainscape*, 1909, oil on canvas, private collection

Exhibition Checklist

Folk Art

Anonymous
Wooden box with painted tassels, 1800–25
Wood, pigment
Collection of Samuel D. and Patricia N.
McCullough

John Brewster, Jr., 1766–1854
Portrait of Rebecca Warren, 1805–10
Oil on canvas
Collection of Samuel D. and Patricia N.
McCullough

Rebecca Warren, 1795–?
Fair Musicians, c. 1805–10
Silk embroidery
Collection of Samuel D. and Patricia N.
McCullough

Thomas Chambers, 1808–69
The Shipwreck, 1850
Oil on canvas
Private collection

Erastus Salisbury Field, 1805–1900
*Pendant Portraits of a Lady and a Gentleman
Seated on a Classical Sofa*, c. 1825–40
Oil on canvas
Collection of Stewart Stender and Deborah
Davenport

William James Hubard, 1807–62
Adam and Eve before the Fall, c. 1840
Oil on canvas
Private collection

Joshua Johnson, 1765–1830
Portrait of Richard John Cock, c. 1815
Oil on canvas
Collection of Samuel D. and Patricia N.
McCullough

Susanna Paine, 1792–1862
Rhode Island Woman in White, 1824
Pastel and applied gold foil on paper
Collection of Stewart Stender and Deborah
Davenport

John Usher Parsons, 1806–74
*Portrait of Mrs. William E. Goodnow
(Harriet Paddleford)*, c. 1837
Oil on canvas
Collection of Samuel D. and Patricia
McCullough

Sheldon Peck, 1797–1868
Captain Forrester of Marblehead, Massachusetts,
1825
Oil on board
Private collection

Sheldon Peck, 1797–1868
Portrait of Oscar Gilbert Adams, c. 1828
Oil on canvas
Collection of Samuel D. and Patricia N.
McCullough

Robert Deacon Peckham, 1785–1877
Portrait of John Adams, c. 1822
Oil on panel
Collection of Samuel D. and Patricia N.
McCullough

Ammi Phillips, 1788–1865
Portrait of Catharina van Keuren, c. 1825
Oil on canvas
Collection of Samuel D. and Patricia N.
McCullough

Susan Catherine Moore Waters, 1823–1900
Boy with Knife, c. 1840–45
Oil on canvas
Collection of Stewart Stender and Deborah
Davenport

Early Minnesota

Anonymous
Fort Snelling, c. 1870–80
Oil on canvas
Collection of Daniel Shogren and Susan Meyer

Grafton Tyler Brown, 1841–1918
Mississippi at Winona, c. 1890
Oil on canvas
Collection of Daniel Shogren and Susan Meyer

James Desvarreaux-Larpenteur, 1847–1937
The Gibbs Homestead, c. 1880
Oil on canvas
Private collection

Seth Eastman, 1808–75
Dacotah Encampment, 1830–31
Watercolor
From the Seth Eastman Collection,
sponsored by Nivin S. MacMillan

Seth Eastman, 1808–75
Falls of St. Anthony, 1851
Watercolor
From the Seth Eastman Collection,
sponsored by Nivin S. MacMillan

Seth Eastman, 1808–75
Indian Courting, n.d.
Watercolor
From the Seth Eastman Collection,
sponsored by Nivin S. MacMillan

Seth Eastman, 1808–75
Indians in Council, 1850
Watercolor
From the Seth Eastman Collection,
sponsored by Nivin S. MacMillan

Seth Eastman, 1808–75
Indian Sugar Camp, n.d.
Watercolor
From the Seth Eastman Collection,
sponsored by Nivin S. MacMillan

Seth Eastman, 1808–75
Indians Traveling, 1850
Watercolor
From the Seth Eastman Collection,
sponsored by Nivin S. MacMillan

Seth Eastman, 1808–75
*Itasca Lake, Source of the Mississippi, 1575 Feet
above the Gulf of Mexico*, n.d.
Watercolor
From the Seth Eastman Collection,
sponsored by Nivin S. MacMillan

Seth Eastman, 1808–75
*Laughing Waters, Three Miles Below the Falls
of St. Anthony*, n.d.
Watercolor
From the Seth Eastman Collection,
sponsored by Nivin S. MacMillan

Seth Eastman, 1808–75
Moccasins, c. 1850
Watercolor on paper
Anonymous lender

Seth Eastman, 1808–75
The Falls of St. Anthony, 1848
Oil on canvas
Anonymous lender

Seth Eastman, 1808–75
*The Mountain that Soaks in the Water (on the
Mississippi, looking South)*, 1848
Watercolor on paper
Anonymous lender

Seth Eastman, 1808–75
Wenona's Leap, Lake Pepin, Mississippi River, 1851
Watercolor
From the Seth Eastman Collection,
sponsored by Nivin S. MacMillan

Seth Eastman, 1808–75
Guarding the Cornfields, n.d.
Watercolor
From the Seth Eastman Collection,
sponsored by Nivin S. MacMillan

Seth Eastman, 1808–75
Marriage Custom of the Indians, n.d.
Watercolor
From the Seth Eastman Collection,
sponsored by Nivin S. MacMillan

Seth Eastman, 1808–75
Gathering Wild Rice, n.d.
Watercolor
From the Seth Eastman Collection,
sponsored by Nivin S. MacMillan

Seth Eastman, 1808–75
Indians Spearing Muskrats in Winter, n.d.
Watercolor
From the Seth Eastman Collection,
sponsored by Nivin S. MacMillan

Barton Stone Hays, 1826–1914
First Mills on the Mississippi and Spirit Island
c. 1857, c. 1880s
Oil on canvas
Anonymous lender

Francis Blackwell Mayer, 1827–99
Little Crow and the Council at Traverse des Sioux,
July 1851, 1897
Oil on canvas
Anonymous lender

Joseph Rusling Meeker, 1827–89
Lake Pepin, 1875
Oil on canvas
Burrichter-Kierlin Collection at the Minnesota
Marine Art Museum, Winona, Minnesota

Edward Kirkbride Thomas, 1817–1906
View of Fort Snelling from Mendota, 1851
Oil on canvas
Anonymous loan

A National Art: Landscape, Still Life, and Genre

Alfred Thompson Bricher, 1837–1908
Mississippi River (Dubuque, Iowa), 1870
Oil on canvas
Burrichter-Kierlin Collection at the Minnesota
Marine Art Museum, Winona, Minnesota

George Loring Brown, 1814–89
The Crown of New England, 1863
Oil on canvas
Collection of Alfred and Ingrid Lenz Harrison

William Mason Brown, 1828–98
Approaching Storm, c. 1870
Oil on canvas
Private collection

Jasper Francis Cropsey, 1823–1900
The Abandoned Skiff, 1882
Oil on canvas
Collection of Alfred and Ingrid Lenz Harrison

Robert Scott Duncanson, 1821–72
Still Life with Fruit and Nuts, 1848
Oil on canvas
Private collection

Asher Brown Durand, 1796–1886
Genesee Valley, New York State, c. 1850
Oil on canvas
Anonymous lender

Asher Brown Durand, 1796–1886
The Peaceful Glen, c. 1858
Oil on canvas
Collection of Douglas and Mary Olson

Alvan Fisher, 1792–1863
Approaching Storm, White Mountains, c. 1820s
Oil on canvas
Anonymous lender

Sanford Robinson Gifford, 1823–80
The Beach at Cohasset, 1864
Oil on paperboard
Private collection

William Michael Harnett, 1848–92
Still Life with Tankard, 1885
Oil on panel
Private collection

William Stanley Haseltine, 1835–1900
Off Newport Island, 1863
Oil on canvas
Burrichter-Kierlin Collection at the Minnesota
Marine Art Museum, Winona, Minnesota

Martin Johnson Heade, 1819–1904
Salt Marsh: Haystacks at Sunset, n.d.
Oil on canvas
Private collection

Winslow Homer, 1836–1910
Prout's Neck in Winter, c. 1892
Oil on canvas
Private collection

Winslow Homer, 1836–1910
Summer Night—Dancing by Moonlight, 1890
Oil on canvas
Anonymous lender

George Inness, 1825–94
Landscape with Sheep, 1858
Oil on canvas
Private collection

George Inness, 1825–94
View near Rome, 1871
Oil on canvas
Collection of John and Elizabeth Driscoll

Eastman Johnson, 1824–1906
Sugaring Off, 1863
Oil on canvas
Private collection

John Frederick Kensett, 1818–72
Beverly Shore, Massachusetts, 1870
Oil on canvas
Anonymous lender

John Frederick Kensett, 1818–72
Border of the Brook, c. 1855–58
Oil on canvas
Collection of Douglas and Mary Olson

John Frederick Kensett, 1818–72
Lily Pond, Rhode Island, 1860
Oil on canvas
Private collection

George Cochran Lambdin, 1830–96
Rose and Ivy, 1875
Oil on panel
Collection of Douglas and Mary Olson

Homer Dodge Martin, 1836–97
White Mountains (Mts. Madison and Adams)
from Mt. Randolph, c. 1862–63
Oil on canvas
Anonymous lender

Homer Dodge Martin, 1836–97
Woodland Waterfall, c. 1890
Oil on canvas
Private collection

Jervis McEntee, 1828–91
Lake Placid—Adirondac, 1868
Oil on canvas
Private collection

Joseph Rusling Meeker, 1827–89
Bayou, n.d.
Oil on canvas
Private collection

Frederick DeBourg Richards, 1822–1903
Untitled (Pastoral Landscape), c. 1880
Oil on canvas
Private collection

William Trost Richards, 1833–1905
Nantucket Bluffs, 1866
Oil on canvas
Collection of Douglas and Mary Olson

Severin Roesen, 1815–72
Fruit Still Life, c. 1860s
Oil on canvas
Collection of Douglas and Mary Olson

Worthington Whittredge, 1820–1910
The Club House Sitting Room at Balsam Lake,
Catskills, New York, 1886
Oil on canvas
Collection of Eleanor and Fred Winston

The Transatlantics: Cosmopolitanism, Expatriates, and American Impressionism

Frank Weston Benson, 1862–1951
Moonlight, 1885
Oil on canvas
Burrichter-Kierlin Collection at the Minnesota
Marine Art Museum, Winona, Minnesota

John Leslie Breck, 1860–99
Farmhouses in Giverny, c. 1880
Oil on canvas
Collection of Michael and Jean Antonello

Theodore Earl Butler, 1861–1936
On the Seine, 1902
Oil on canvas
Private collection

William Merritt Chase, 1849–1916
Prospect Park, Brooklyn, c. 1886
Oil on canvas
Antonello Family Foundation

Dawson Dawson-Watson, 1864–1939
Haystacks, Giverny, c. 1890
Oil on canvas
Collection of Michael and Jean Antonello

Childe Hassam, 1859–1935
Sixth Avenue El—Nocturne (The El, New York),
1894
Oil on canvas
Collection of Michael and Jean Antonello

Childe Hassam, 1859–1935
Woman in a Flower Garden, c. 1890–91
Oil on canvas
Collection of Michael and Jean Antonello

George Hitchcock, 1850–1913
Swans by a Bridge, Holland, 1898
Oil on canvas
Collection of Siri and Bob Marshall

Walter Launt Palmer, 1854–1932
Blue-Barred Snow, 1888
Oil on canvas
Collection of Alfred and Ingrid Lenz Harrison

Walter Launt Palmer, 1854–1932
Lagoon of Venice, 1895
Oil on canvas
Private collection

William Lamb Picknell, 1853–97
Moret on the Loing River, c. 1896
Oil on canvas
Anonymous lender

Charles Adam Platt, 1861–1933
Larmor at Low Tide, 1885
Oil on canvas
Anonymous lender

Hiram Powers, 1805–73
Charity, 1867–71
Marble
Antonello Family Foundation

Hiram Powers, 1805–73
Faith, 1866
Marble
Antonello Family Foundation

Hiram Powers, 1805–73
Hope, 1866–67
Marble
Antonello Family Foundation

Robert Lewis Reid, 1862–1929
Girl at Window, 1885
Oil on canvas
Collection of Siri and Bob Marshall

Theodore Robinson, 1852–96
Farm among Hills, Giverny, c. 1890
Oil on canvas
Anonymous lender

Theodore Robinson, 1852–96
Normandy Farm, c. 1891
Oil on canvas
Collection of Michael and Jean Antonello

Theodore Robinson, 1852–96
The Plum Tree, c. 1890–96
Oil on canvas
Collection of Michael and Jean Antonello

John Singer Sargent, 1856–1925
Jerusalem, 1906
Oil on canvas
Private collection

John Singer Sargent, 1856–1925
The Moraine, 1908
Oil on canvas
Private collection

John Singer Sargent, 1856–1925
Study of a Salmon, c. 1902
Watercolor on paper, over preliminary pencil
Collection of Michael and Jean Antonello

John Singer Sargent, 1856–1925
Val d'Aosta: Stepping Stones, c. 1907
Oil on canvas
Collection of Michael and Jean Antonello

John Singer Sargent, 1856–1925
Venetian Canal, n.d.
Watercolor and pencil on paper
Collection of Michael and Jean Antonello

Edmund Charles Tarbell, 1862–1938
Emeline, in a Garden, c. 1890
Oil on canvas
Collection of Michael and Jean Antonello

Edmund Charles Tarbell, 1862–1938
Portrait of Mercie Tarbell, c. 1919
Oil on canvas
Private collection

Robert William Vonnoh, 1858–1933
Study for the Ring, c. 1891
Oil on canvas
Collection of Michael and Jean Antonello

James Abbott McNeill Whistler, 1834–1903
The Widow (Beatrice Philip Godwin Whistler),
c. 1887
Oil on canvas
Anonymous lender

James Abbott McNeill Whistler, 1834–1903
Howth Head, near Dublin, 1900
Oil on panel
Anonymous lender

James Abbott McNeill Whistler, 1834–1903
The Seashore, 1883–85
Oil on panel
Anonymous lender

James Abbott McNeill Whistler, 1834–1903
Venetian Courtyard: Court of Palazzo Zorzi,
1879–80
Pastel on brown paper
Anonymous lender

Tonalism

Ralph Albert Blakelock, 1847–1919
Moonlight, n.d.
Oil on canvas
Collection of John and Elizabeth Driscoll

Arthur Bowen Davies, 1862–1928
The Nearer Forest, 1905
Oil on canvas
Private collection

William Crothers Fitler, 1857–1915
Sunset Hour (New York Landscape), n.d.
Oil on canvas
Collection of Billie Lawton

Benjamin Foster, 1852–1926
Connecticut Landscape, n.d.
Oil on canvas
Lent by Paul and Barbara Watkins

George Inness, 1825–94
Sunset at Montclair, 1892
Oil on canvas backed by panel
Collection of John and Elizabeth Driscoll

George Inness, 1825–94
The Triumph at Calvary, c. 1874
Oil on canvas
Collection of Andrew Fuller

George Inness, 1825–94
Two Rainbows, Montclair, 1892
Oil on canvas
Collection of Daniel T. and Helen E. Lindsay

Homer Dodge Martin, 1836–97
Westchester Hills, c. 1887
Oil on canvas
Anonymous lender

John Francis Murphy, 1853–1921
Afternoon Light, 1887
Oil on canvas
Collection of John and Elizabeth Driscoll

John Francis Murphy, 1853–1921
Falling Leaves, n.d.
Oil on canvas
Anonymous lender

John Francis Murphy, 1853–1921
Sunset Landscape, 1893
Oil on canvas
Lent by Paul and Barbara Watkins

Dwight William Tryon, 1849–1925
Early Moonrise—October, 1913–14
Oil on canvas
Collection of Douglas and Mary Olson

Alexander Helwig Wyant, 1836–92
Clouds and Sunshine, n.d.
Oil on canvas
Collection of John and Elizabeth Driscoll

Minnesota Painters

Nicholas Richard Brewer, 1857–1949
At the Spring, c. 1895
Oil on canvas
Promised gift of Rob P. Stock in memory
of his parents, Philip E. and Mary C.
(Mathewson) Stock

Nicholas Richard Brewer, 1857–1949
The Shadow of the Grove, 1910
Oil on canvas
Collection of Stephen J. Brewer

Nicholas Richard Brewer, 1857–1949
Winter on the Mississippi, 1909
Oil on canvas
Collection of Jeffrey C. Meehan

David Ericson, 1873–1946
Near Dordrecht, c. 1901–12
Oil on canvas
Anonymous lender

Alexis Jean Fournier, 1865–1948
A Minnesota Sunset, 1889
Oil on canvas
Anonymous lender

Alexis Jean Fournier, 1865–1948
After Rain, c. 1902
Oil on canvas
Private collection

Alexis Jean Fournier, 1865–1948
Burton Farm, Deephaven, Minnesota, October 17, 1890, 1890
Charcoal on paper
Lent by Durand and Mary Sue Potter

Alexis Jean Fournier, 1865–1948
Cazin's Cottage, Normandy, c. 1907
Color monotype on paper
Collection of Sheila Morgan

Alexis Jean Fournier, 1865–1948
In Daubigny's Country: Chaponval, France, 1912
Oil on canvas
MPB Collection

Alexis Jean Fournier, 1865–1948
Mill Pond, Pine Island, Minnesota, c. 1885–86
Oil on artist board
Collection of Jeffrey C. Meehan

Alexis Jean Fournier, 1865–1948
Minnesota Scene, 1892
Oil on canvas
MPB Collection

Alexis Jean Fournier, 1865–1948
Off the Coast (Lake Superior), 1886
Oil on canvas
Collection of Sheila Morgan

Alexis Jean Fournier, 1865–1948
Old Mill Ruins at Pine Island, Minnesota,
c. 1885–86
Oil on artist board
Collection of Jeffrey C. Meehan

Alexis Jean Fournier, 1865–1948
Old Row (Fort Snelling) *from the Station,
July 1888*, 1888
Oil on canvas
Anonymous lender

Alexis Jean Fournier, 1865–1948
Passing Storm, 1907
Monotype on paper
MPB Collection

Alexis Jean Fournier, 1865–1948
Snow Scene (Rooftops), c. 1903
Oil on canvas
Private collection

Alexis Jean Fournier, 1865–1948
Solitude at Night, 1912
Oil on canvas board
Anonymous lender

Alexis Jean Fournier, 1865–1948
The Old Swimming Hole, c. 1903
Monotype on paper
Collection of Billie Lawton

Alexis Jean Fournier, 1865–1948
Trout Brook, Connecticut, 1916
Oil on canvas board
Anonymous lender

Alexis Jean Fournier, 1865–1948
Untitled, October 9, 1891, 1891
Charcoal on paper
Lent by Durand and Mary Sue Potter

Alexis Jean Fournier, 1865–1948
*Virginia around the Bend at the Confluence of the
Mississippi and Minnesota Rivers*, 1889
Oil on canvas
Anonymous lender

Herbjørn Gausta, 1854–1924
Moonlit Scene, c. 1908
Oil on canvas
Private collection

Alexander Grinager, 1865–1949
The Fountain, n.d.
Oil on canvas
Collection of Sheila Morgan

Alexander Grinager, 1865–1949
Wild Minnie, c. 1890s
Oil on canvas
Private collection

Knute Heldner, 1877–1952
Birches, c. 1910s
Oil on canvas
Anonymous lender

Robert Koehler, 1850–1917
Minnehaha Creek, c. 1910
Watercolor on paper
MPB Collection

Robert Koehler, 1850–1917
Stoney Point, Lake Ida (Douglas County,
Minnesota), c. 1900
Oil on canvas
Private collection

Douglas Volk, 1856–1935
View of a Country Village, c. 1880
Oil on canvas
Collection of Jeffrey C. Meehan

On the Cusp of Modernism

George Wesley Bellows, 1882–1925
Gull Rock—Whitehead, 1911
Oil on panel
Private collection

George Wesley Bellows, 1882–1925
Upper Broadway, 1907
Oil on board
Collection of Michael and Jean Antonello

William James Glackens, 1870–1938
Portsmouth Harbor, 1909
Oil on canvas
Burrichter-Kierlin Collection at the Minnesota
Marine Art Museum, Winona, Minnesota

Marsden Hartley, 1877–1943
An Evening Mountainscape, 1909
Oil on canvas
Private collection

Leon Kroll, 1884–1974
On the Hudson, c. 1910
Oil on panel
Anonymous lender

Walt Francis Kuhn, 1877–1949
Woman in Red Scarf near Seashore, n.d.
Oil on canvas
Collection of Alfred and Ingrid Lenz Harrison

Ernest Lawson, 1873–1939
New Hope, Pennsylvania, n.d.
Oil on board
Collection of Michael and Jean Antonello

George Benjamin Luks, 1867–1933
Leena (William Glackens's daughter), 1910
Oil on board
Collection of Michael and Jean Antonello

John Marin, 1870–1953
Region Weehauken, New Jersey, 1903–4
Oil on canvas
Collection of John and Elizabeth Driscoll

Maurice Brazil Prendergast, 1858–1924
The Bartol Church (The Fountain), 1900–1901
Watercolor and pencil on paper
Antonello Family Foundation

Maurice Brazil Prendergast, 1858–1924
Elegant Woman in Blue Dress, c. 1893–94
Watercolor and pencil on paper
Antonello Family Foundation

John French Sloan, 1871–1951
Gloucester, c. 1914
Oil on canvas
Collection of John and Elizabeth Driscoll

John French Sloan, 1871–1951
New York Street after the Snow, c. 1903–5
Oil on canvas
Private collection

Eduard Jean Steichen, 1879–1973
Mountain of the Crouching Lion, 1916
Oil on board
Private collection